WRITE
EVERY TIME
(Or Is That 'RIGHT'?)

Cool Ways to
Improve Your English

Written by Lottie Stride
Illustrated by Andrew Pinder

Edited by Elizabeth Scoggins
Designed by Zoe Quayle

WRITE
EVERY TIME
(Or Is That 'RIGHT'?)

Cool Ways to
Improve Your English

Buster Books

First published in Great Britain in 2010 by Buster Books,
an imprint of Michael O'Mara Books Limited,
9 Lion Yard, Tremadoc Road, London SW4 7NQ

www.mombooks.com/busterbooks

Copyright © Buster Books 2010
Cover designed by Angie Allison

A CIP catalogue record for this book is available from the British Library.

ISBN: 978-1-907151-15-6

1 3 5 7 9 10 8 6 4 2

Papers used by Michael O'Mara Books are natural, recyclable products
made from wood grown in sustainable forests. The manufacturing processes
conform to the environmental regulations of the country of origin.

Printed and bound in July 2010 by Clays Limited, St Ives plc, Popson Street,
Bungay, Suffolk, NR35 1ED, UK.

CONTENTS

ALL ABOUT
THIS BOOK

Need a bit of grammar guidance? Want to be superb at spelling? Struggling with your full stops and commas? Then this is the book you need. It's packed with lots of helpful information and top tips to help you sort out your grammar, spelling and punctuation.

Whether you're writing a letter to a friend, finishing your first novel, or perhaps one day filling in an application for your dream job – the more you understand how to use English, the better you'll do.

More Words, Please!

You probably know that a group of sheep is called a 'flock', but have you ever heard of a 'storytelling' of rooks or an 'ostentation' of peacocks?

The English language is packed with more words than almost any other, which means there's a word for practically everything. For example, if your writing is already super-slick and simply sensational there's a name for the kind of words you are choosing: it's alliteration. See?

How This Book Works

Each section is divided into bite-sized chunks that will make tackling any part of the English language simple. You can dip in and out of the things you need help with, or read the whole book from beginning to end, with breaks, of course!

If you need to look back at anything another time, there's an index at the back of the book to help you find it.

What's In Store?

Throughout this book there are all sorts of interesting facts about the language you speak.

You'll discover which countries gave us the words 'pyjamas' and 'canoe'; why 'practice' and 'practise' aren't quite the same thing; that 'would of' doesn't mean anything; where in a sentence a comma should go; and how to avoid accidents like this:

If the children don't finish their chips put them in the bin.

Before you know it, you'll be writing with a flourish, spelling like a champion and punctuating perfectly, with a head full of great ways to help you improve your writing, stun your teachers and much, much more.

GOODNESS GRACIOUS GRAMMAR

_____GETTING STARTED_____

You use grammar every time you read or write or speak. Grammar gives you all the rules about how to put words together in sentences. Using the right grammar helps other people to understand what you mean.

You can make short, sharp sentences, like this:

> "Get lost," she snapped.

You can be poetic:

> The crafty creature slowly crept; the terrified child shivered and wept …

And you can inform:

> The two-toed sloth is a tree-dwelling tropical mammal not noted for its speed.

Extra Information

Grammar Extra. Throughout this section, you'll find 'Grammar Extras' that give you more detail on the subject you have just read about – these will really help you impress your teachers!

Grammar Guidance. These will give you useful tips and suggestions that will come in handy when you put grammar into practice.

Did You Know? Lastly, you'll find extra bits of information under the 'Did You Know?' headings – interesting stuff ranging from the weird to the wonderful.

THE PARTS OF SPEECH

Every type of word in a sentence has a name and these names are known as the 'parts of speech'. This poem gives you a handy reminder of each of them:

> Every name is called a **noun**,
> As field and fountain, street and town.
> In place of noun the **pronoun** stands
> As he and she can clap their hands.
> The **adjective** describes a thing,
> As magic wand and bridal ring.
> The **verb** means action, something done –
> To read, to write, to jump, to run.
> How things are done, the **adverbs** tell,
> As quickly, slowly, badly, well.
> The **preposition** shows relation,
> As in the street, or at the station.
> **Conjunctions** join, in many ways,
> Sentences, words, or phrase and phrase.
> The **interjection** cries out, "Hark!
> I need an exclamation mark!"
> Through poetry, we learn how each
> Of these make up the **parts of speech**.

The information on the following pages tells you more about the parts of speech.

HOW ABOUT NOUNS?

A noun is a name for a thing, a person or a place. Words such as 'bus', 'chair', 'dragon', 'firework', 'hosepipe', 'maggot', 'octópus', 'teacher' and 'tree' are all nouns.

Common Nouns

There are different types of noun and the easiest type to spot are called 'common nouns'. These are names for ordinary things, such as a book, a box or a button. They are also names for less ordinary things, such as a platypus, an asteroid or an earthquake, but they are all still common nouns. Remember, if you can put 'the', 'a' or 'an' in front of a word, it is probably a common noun.

Grammar Extra

'The', 'a' and 'an' are short words with long names in grammar. They are known as the 'definite article' (the) and the 'indefinite article' (a and an).

If you say *a* man, you are talking about *any* man. If you say *the* man, you are talking about a particular man – a *definite* man.

A MAN

THE MAN

Proper Nouns

Some nouns start with a capital letter. These are called proper nouns. They name one specific thing, such as a particular person or a particular country. Your name is a proper noun and so is the name of the country in which you live. Here are some more examples of proper nouns, followed by the matching common noun:

Proper Noun	(Common Noun)
William	(boy)
Potter	(surname)
Norway	(country)
Friday	(day)
October	(month)

Did You Know?

The word 'sandwich' is a common noun these days, but it didn't start out that way. Legend has it that a tasty snack of meat placed between two pieces of bread was created for the Earl of Sandwich – Sandwich is a place in England, so it is a proper noun in this case – and named after him.

The words 'cardigan', 'leotard', 'mac' and 'silhouette' were people's names, and so were once proper nouns, too.

Abstract Nouns

The word 'abstract' describes something that is an idea rather than an object. Abstract nouns are words that describe things, but not things that actually exist as objects. You can't see them or hear them, and you can't touch, smell or taste them either.

'Excitement', 'failure', 'friendship', 'generosity', 'impatience', 'poverty', 'sleep', 'success' and 'virtue' are all abstract nouns.

Collective Nouns

'Collective nouns' describe groups of people or things. For example, a class is a group of school children, an army is a group of soldiers, and a deck is a group of cards. 'Audience', 'bunch', 'collection', 'family', 'jury', 'orchestra', 'parliament' and 'team' are all collective nouns.

Did You Know?

There are lots of collective nouns for animals, too. You probably know some of the ordinary ones, such as a flock of sheep or a herd of cows, but how about these particularly unusual ones?

a *business* of ferrets
an *intrusion* of cockroaches
a *descent* of woodpeckers
a *labour* of moles
a *pod* of dolphins
a *shiver* of sharks
a *wake* of buzzards
an *unkindness* of ravens
a *storytelling* of rooks
a *murder* of crows
an *ostentation* of peacocks.

PUT PRONOUNS IN

'Pronouns' are words which are used as stand-ins for nouns. This means that you can use them instead of nouns to really liven up your speaking or writing. Try reading this:

> Lucy spotted a sea monster. The sea monster had enormous horns and the sea monster was swimming straight towards Lucy. Lucy couldn't outswim the sea monster. Could Lucy tame the sea monster, or hypnotize the sea monster? The sea monster was getting nearer. The sea monster's huge mouth opened in a roar. Help! The sea monster was going to eat Lucy ... Then Lucy woke up.

It's a bit repetitive, isn't it? Now see what happens when you put some pronouns in:

Lucy spotted a sea monster. It had enormous horns and it was swimming straight towards her. She couldn't outswim it. Could she tame it, or hypnotize it? It was getting nearer. Its huge mouth opened in a roar. Help! The sea monster was going to eat her… Then Lucy woke up.

See how much snappier it is, thanks to a few pronouns? In the paragraph above, 'it', 'she' and 'her' are all pronouns.

What's Mine Is Yours

The words listed below are called 'personal pronouns'. The words in the first column are pronouns that you can use as the subject of a sentence. The pronouns in the second column can be used as the object in a sentence. (See pages 44 to 48 for more on subjects and objects.) The third column contains 'possessive' pronouns. These are used to show that something belongs to someone – or to several people:

Subject	Object	Possessive
I	me	mine
you	you	yours
he	him	his
she	her	hers
it	it	its
we	us	ours
you (plural)	you	yours
they	them	theirs

Grammar Guidance. Avoid using a pronoun if it makes the meaning of your sentence unclear. For example:

If the children don't finish their chips, put them in the bin.

Will the chips or the children end up in the bin?

_FURTHER PRONOUNS____

Lots of different words can act as pronouns, and they have many different jobs – here are just a few of them.

Relative Pronouns

The words 'that', 'which', 'who', 'whom' and 'whose' can be used as 'relative pronouns'. These are words that connect two parts of a sentence and describe the relationship between the two parts. For example:

> This is the boy *who* took my lolly.
> Where is the ball *which* I kicked over the fence?

Grammar Guidance. You can only use 'who' in relation to people and 'which' in relation to animals or things. However, in general, 'that' can be used for either.

Reflexive Pronouns

The words 'myself', 'yourself', 'himself', 'herself', 'itself', 'ourselves', 'yourselves' and 'themselves' are called reflexive pronouns. A reflexive pronoun allows you to refer back to a person or thing that you have already mentioned.

Subject	Reflexive Pronoun
I	myself
you	yourself
he	himself
she	herself
it	itself
we	ourselves
you	yourselves
they	themselves

You use a reflexive pronoun when a sentence has the same subject and object in it, like this:

> I can look after myself.

In this sentence, *I* is the subject, *myself* is the object.

Grammar Guidance. Be careful. Sometimes a reflexive pronoun can change the meaning of a sentence completely:

Tom's teacher was extremely pleased with him.

Tom's teacher was extremely pleased with *himself*.

Spot the difference?

ADDED EXTRAS

Sometimes a noun on its own just doesn't give you enough detail – you want to add information. To add information to a noun, you use a word called an 'adjective'. Think of it as an added extra that describes the noun.

Using Adjectives

Suppose you have to describe a building, and you want to tell people what the building is like – you'll need to use adjectives. You might describe an old, ruined building, or a scary, abandoned building. 'Old', 'ruined', 'scary' and 'abandoned' are all adjectives.

Grammar Guidance. An adjective goes before the noun it is describing, like this:

a *blue* moon
a *gorgeous* girl
a *grumpy* teacher
the *top* floor
an *ugly* bug.

Small, Smaller, Smallest ...

Some adjectives can be used to make a comparison. There are two kinds – a 'comparative' one and a 'superlative' one. Use the comparative when you compare two things, for example:

My pudding is *smaller* than yours.

A comparative adjective always goes hand in hand with 'than'.

You should use a superlative adjective when you are comparing several things, as in:

My pudding is *smallest* out of all three.

Here are some more examples:

Adjective	Comparative	Superlative
small	smaller	smallest
big	bigger	biggest
large	larger	largest
narrow	narrower	narrowest
pale	paler	palest
rich	richer	richest
easy	easier	easiest.

Grammar Guidance. Adjectives that have more than two syllables (see page 61 for more on these), such as 'beautiful' and 'popular', do not follow the same rule. For example, there's no such thing as 'beautifuller' and 'beautifullest'. For these adjectives, you should always use the words 'more' and 'than' to make your comparison. For example:

Your painting is *more* beautiful than mine.

To make the superlative, you should use 'most':

Your painting is the *most* beautiful out of everyone's.

This rule also works for any adjective ending in '-ous', '-ing' or '-ed', such as 'famous', 'boring' or 'excited'.

Rule-Breakers

Lastly, there are a few adjectives which break all the rules. Here are a few examples:

Adjective	Comparative	Superlative
bad	worse	worst
good	better	best
little	less	least
fun	more fun	most fun
many	more	most
much	more	most.

ADVANCE ON VERBS

'Verbs' are doing words. 'Cry', 'do', 'go', 'have', 'laugh', 'like', 'run', 'skip', 'speak', 'splutter', 'tell', 'try', 'wish' – these are all verbs. They describe the actions of someone or something in a sentence. Without a verb, you don't have a sentence:

> Jason a mountain.
> Lucy her violin.
> Cats mice.

See? You need to add a verb to make each group of words make sense. For instance:

> Jason *climbed* a mountain.
> Lucy *plays* her violin.
> Cats *chase* mice.

Verbs in their simplest form, used with the word 'to', are known as infinitives. 'To speak' and 'to run', for example, are the infinitives of the verbs 'speak' and 'run' – you will often use an infinitive with another verb, like this:

> I *like* to run.
> I *want* to speak.

With Or Without?

Some verbs can work well with just a subject noun (see pages 44 to 46 for more on these). The following sentences make perfect sense by themselves:

> Babies chuckle.
> Toast burns.

However, many verbs need an object noun, or they don't make much sense at all. For instance, 'I buy' and 'I get' don't tell you anything on their own – you need more detail:

> I buy a ticket.
> I get a train.

Grammar Guidance. There are lots of short verbs that you use all the time, such as 'come', 'do', 'go', 'see', 'say', 'run' and 'walk'. However, when you're building a sentence, you can have fun thinking about which other verbs to use instead.

Not Now!

Negative words, such as 'not' and 'neither', will give a sentence the opposite meaning. For example:

> I *do not* want to speak.

However, two negatives in a sentence contradict each other. 'I *don't* like running *neither*,' for example, means you *do* like running. This is known as a double negative and should be avoided.

Lost For Words?

One of the great things about the English language is that there are so many different choices. How about using any of the following words in place of 'speak', for instance?

> chatter
> gabble
> grumble
> jabber
> mutter
> prattle
> whisper.

Or these in place of 'run'?

> bound
> dash
> hurtle
> lope
> rush
> scamper
> scarper.

If you are ever stuck for a replacement word, you can use a special kind of dictionary called a 'thesaurus'. In a thesaurus, words with similar meanings, or 'synonyms' (see page 55), are arranged in groups, so that an alternative word is always at the tip of your fingers.

PAST, PRESENT, FUTURE

If you want to describe *when* things are taking place, it's the verb in your sentence that helps you. You can change when an action happens by changing the 'tense' of the verb.

Tense Times

Tenses can tell you if something has happened in the *past*, will happen in the *future* or is happening *right now*. You can tell your readers if a sentence is talking about the past, the present or the future by adding a different ending to the verb. You can also add a helper word, called an auxiliary verb, such as 'will', 'shall' or 'am' to help you be more specific about when the action is taking place (see pages 26 to 31 for more on these).

Each tense has a different name. However, these names are less important than knowing when to use each form of the verb, so that what you say and write is as clear as possible.

'To Be' And 'To Have'

The two verbs you use more than any other are 'to be' and 'to have'. You often use them to describe things or to ask questions. These sentences all use different forms of the verbs 'to be' and 'to have':

> I *am* cold.
> She *is* tall.
> *Are* you hungry?
> I *have* blue eyes.
> Who *has* my pen?

Here they are in each of their simplest forms in the present and past tenses:

(To Be)		(To Have)	
Present	Past	Present	Past
I am	I was	I have	I had
you are	you were	you have	you had
he/she/it is	he/she/it was	he/she/it has	he/she/it had
we are	we were	we have	we had
you are	you were	you have	you had
they are	they were.	they have	they had.

As well as acting quite happily by themselves, 'to be' and 'to have' also play an important role in forming different tenses, when they act as auxiliary verbs, helping other verbs to be more specific (see pages 26 to 31).

Grammar Extra

You are almost never allowed to say 'I were' instead of 'I was', except when you are imagining or wishing a different situation to the one you are in. For example, 'If I were rich.'

Present Tense

There are two main versions of the present tense. The simple present tense uses the main verb without 'to' at the beginning:

> I play tennis.
> You play tennis.
> He/she/it plays tennis.
> We play tennis.
> You play tennis.
> They play tennis.

Note that you add an **s** on the end of the verb when you are talking about 'he', 'she' or 'it'.

With some verbs, such as 'wish', for example, you'll need to add '-es' for 'he', 'she' and 'it' – 'wishes'.

The simple present tense can be used for all sorts of things, such as facts (you *write* neatly), and to talk about things that you do regularly (I *play* tennis).

Keep Going

To say that something is happening right now, you need the 'present continuous' tense. This tells you that the action is taking place right now and continuing.

You use it all the time by adding an auxiliary verb – in this case, the present form of the verb 'to be' ('am', 'are', 'is') – followed by what is called the 'present participle' of the verb you are using. The present participle is always made from the main verb with '-ing' added on the end:

> I *am playing* tennis.
> You *are playing* tennis.
> He/she/it *is playing* tennis.
> We *are playing* tennis.
> You *are playing* tennis.
> They *are playing* tennis.

Past Tense

To move the action in your sentence into the past, you can use the simple past tense.

Do this by adding what is called the 'past participle', usually '-ed', to the end of the main verb:

> I *played* tennis.
> You *played* tennis.
> He/she/it *played* tennis.
> We *played* tennis.
> You *played* tennis.
> They *played* tennis.

There are also other 'irregular' past participles, including '-n', as in show*n,* and '-t', as in learn*t,* as well as lots of irregular verbs that don't obey the rules and do their own thing (see pages 32 to 33).

Keep Going In The Past

You can also use the verb 'to be' in its past tense ('was' or 'were') as an auxiliary verb, together with an -ing verb. This makes the 'past continuous' tense, which tells you that something took place over a period of time:

> I *was playing* tennis.
> You *were playing* tennis.
> He/she/it *was playing* tennis.
> We *were playing* tennis.
> You *were playing* tennis.
> They *were playing* tennis.

Past Tense Extra

There are all sorts of other ways of talking about the past, too. The 'past perfect' tense, for instance, is formed using the past tense form of 'to have' ('had') and another verb with its past participle.

It tells you about a situation in the past that was caused by something that happened earlier. For example, the sentence:

> When I came home, they *had eaten* all the cake.

tells you that there was no cake left for you, because it had been eaten.

You can even tell people that you did something for a while, but don't any more by adding the words 'used to':

> I *used to* play tennis.

This lets everyone know that you no longer play tennis.

Future Tense

Although there isn't a future participle like there is for the present and past tense, there are still lots of ways to put the action you are speaking or writing about into the future.

One of the most common ways of making the future tense is to use the auxiliary verbs 'shall' or 'will', followed by another verb – 'play' for instance. Traditionally, you should use 'shall' for 'I' and 'we', and 'will' for all the other people, like this:

I *shall play*.
You *will play*.
He/she/it *will play*.
We *shall play*.
You *will play*.
They *will play*.

Keep Going In The Future

You can make a 'continuous future' tense along with the verb 'to be' as an auxiliary verb, just like you would in the present and past tenses. This tells you that something is taking place over a period of time in the future:

> I *shall be playing*.
> You *will be playing*.
> He/she/it *will be playing*.
> We *shall be playing*.
> You *will be playing*.
> They *will be playing*.

Future Tense Extra

There are lots of other ways you can talk about the future, too. All you need is a selection of auxiliary verbs to help things along. For example:

> I *am going to buy* shoes tomorrow.
> You *will win* the race.
> It *will be* sunny tomorrow.
> We *shall be going* to school tomorrow.
> You *are coming* with us tonight.
> They *will be* here in a minute.

More On Auxiliary Verbs

You've already come across 'to be' and 'to have', and 'shall' and 'will' as auxiliary verbs, but these are not the only ones. The following words can all be used to help change the meaning of another verb:

> could, should, would,
> do, does, did,
> may, might, must.

You can even combine them with 'to be' and 'to have' to explain a huge amount more about the verb:

> I *might have been* chosen, but I was ill.
> My top *could be being* crumpled as it's in a suitcase.

Grammar Guidance. What's wrong with this sentence?

> I would of liked an ice cream.

That's right, 'of' is a preposition (see page 37) – there is no verb 'to of', ever. The full sentence should be:

> I *would have* liked an ice cream.

This can be shortened to:

> I *would've* liked an ice cream.

A REGULAR REBELLION

Some verbs, such as 'to like', are known as regular verbs. They work quite straightforwardly when you change the tense they are in:

Present	Past	Future
I like	I liked	I shall like
you like	you liked	you will like
he/she/it likes	he/she/it liked	he/she/it will like
we like	we liked	we shall like
you like	you liked	you will like
they like	they liked	they will like.

However, some verbs are irregular – they don't behave so predictably. Use the table opposite to get a good idea of how lots of verbs change from their present tense form to the simple past. You can also see each of their past participles – the words that would usually end in '-ed', as in 'liked'.

Irregular Verb Table

Simple Present	Simple Past	Past Participle
awake	awoke	awoken
be	was or were	been
begin	began	begun
bring	brought	brought
buy	bought	bought
choose	chose	chosen
come	came	come
do	did	done
draw	drew	drawn
eat	ate	eaten
feel	felt	felt
find	found	found
forget	forgot	forgotten
give	gave	given
go	went	gone
grow	grew	grown
have	had	had
hear	heard	heard
know	knew	known
leave	left	left
lose	lost	lost
make	made	made
read	read	read
run	ran	run
say	said	said
see	saw	seen
speak	spoke	spoken
swim	swam	swum
take	took	taken
teach	taught	taught
think	thought	thought
understand	understood	understood
wear	wore	worn
win	won	won
write	wrote	written.

ALL ABOUT ADVERBS

'Adverbs' explain more about a verb. In the same way that an adjective gives extra information about a noun, an adverb gives you more detail about a verb.

Take this sentence:

I eat.

This is fine on its own, but everyone eats, don't they? To give more detail, use an adverb to make it clear just how you eat:

I eat *quickly.*
I eat *greedily.*
I eat *slowly.*

Each of the following words is an adverb and, as you can see, a lot of adverbs end in '-ly':

angrily	nosily
bumpily	oddly
cautiously	perkily
dreamily	quietly
energetically	rashly
furiously	sensibly
gingerly	truthfully
happily	unhelpfully
idiotically	viciously
jerkily	weakly
kindly	xenophobically*
loyally	yappily
mischievously	zanily.

* See page 69 to find out more about using a dictionary to look up the meaning of unfamiliar words.

34

Grammar Guidance. Don't be tricked into thinking that all adverbs end in '-ly'. Those aren't the only ones. Here are a few that you might use quite a lot:

> almost
> fast
> hard
> never
> once
> soon
> twice
> well.

There are also lots of words ending in '-ly' that aren't adverbs. For example, in the sentence:

> Hedgehogs are prickly.

TELL ME ABOUT IT!

The word 'prickly' isn't an adverb. It's an adjective describing hedgehogs. It's easy to confuse an adverb with a different kind of word ending in '-ly', but if you can't work out which it is, try changing the verb to see if it still makes sense:

> Hedgehogs *walk* prickly.

This doesn't make sense, so 'prickly' isn't an adverb.

Double Duty

Some words can be used as an adjective *and* as an adverb:

> Cheetahs are fast.
> I ran fast.

'Fast' is an adjective when it's telling you more about the noun 'cheetahs'. It's an adverb when it's telling you more about the verb 'ran'.

Where Did I Put My Adverb?

It often doesn't matter where you put an adverb in a sentence because its meaning still stays the same:

> She spoke *hesitantly*.
> *Hesitantly*, she spoke.
> She *hesitantly* spoke.

However, you can sometimes make some important changes if you're not careful. For instance, these two sentences have a subtle, but distinctly different sense:

> Idiotically, she was dancing on the cliff edge.
> She was dancing idiotically on the cliff edge.

Depending on where you put them, some adverbs, such as 'even', 'only', 'almost', 'also', 'just' and 'mainly', can make changes to the meaning of your sentence. For example, each of these sentences has a slightly different meaning:

> Only I gave my brother a pencil.
> I only gave my brother a pencil.
> I gave only my brother a pencil.
> I gave my brother only a pencil.

_____IT'S BEHIND YOU!___

Prepositions are words that show how one thing is connected to another, as in 'at', 'by', 'in', 'of', 'off' and 'up'. They describe the position of things, and usually go before a noun or a pronoun. For example:

The baby was *in* the bath.
The house was *by* a river.
I whizzed *down* the waterslide.

You use prepositions all the time when you're speaking and writing:

I wanted to stay *in* bed, but Mum made me go *to* school. I got *in* trouble for laughing *in* maths. *In* PE I fell *off* the wallbars and went somersaulting *across* the gym. Some days it's just not worth getting *up* in the first place.

Sometimes a group of words can make a preposition, too:

> away from
> far from
> in front of
> near to
> next to
> out of.

Grammar Guidance. Try to avoid using more prepositions than you need though, such as 'of' in this sentence:

> I got off *of* the bus.

CONJUNCTION ZONE

'Conjunctions' are words that you use to join things together, as in 'and', 'or', 'but' and 'so'. You can join words, clauses or phrases with them (see pages 47 to 49 for more on these). They make your writing flow much more smoothly. Read this example:

> I met a grumpy fairy. She gave me a wish. I wished for wings. The wings appeared. They were useless. They were shimmery. They were sparkly. They were fairy-sized. They were also stuck to my shoulders. "You wished for wings. You got them," snapped the fairy. The fairy disappeared.

It's a bit jerky, isn't it?

Try this instead:

> I met a grumpy fairy. She gave me a wish, *so* I wished for wings. The wings appeared *but* they were useless. They were shimmery *and* sparkly *and* fairy-sized. They were also stuck to my shoulders. "You wished for wings. You got them," snapped the fairy *and* disappeared.

Get Co-ordinated!

The words 'and', 'nor', 'but', 'or', 'yet' and 'so' are known as co-ordinating conjunctions. You use them to join words, sentences, or parts of sentences that are equally important.

For example, 'Cats like to miaow.' and, 'Dogs like to bark.' are equally important, so you can connect them with a co-ordinating conjunction, like this:

Cats like to miaow, *and* dogs like to bark.

Or like this:

Cats like to miaow, *but* dogs like to bark.

You can often change the meaning of a sentence with the conjunction you choose, like this:

Cats like to miaow, *so* dogs like to bark.

This would mean that dogs like to bark *because* cats like to miaow.

Grammar Guidance. If you are joining two sentences that contain the same noun, you can take the second noun away to avoid repetition. For example, if you join, 'The toddler fell over' with, 'The toddler started bawling' you can say:

The toddler fell over and started bawling.

Rather than:

The toddler fell over and the toddler started bawling.

Grammar Extra

Usually, it's best to avoid starting a sentence with a conjunction, especially if you are writing a formal letter or if you're doing school work. However, it is perfectly all right to start a sentence with 'and' or 'but' in stories or in informal writing. You will probably notice that lots of writers use these words for dramatic effect and for emphasis. And you can, too! It can work well so long as you don't overdo it.

CONJUNCTION EXTRAS

There are three other types of conjunction as well as co-ordinating conjunctions. These are:

Subordinate

Subordinate conjunctions join the more important clause to the less important clause – its subordinate (see pages 47 to 48). They are words such as 'although', 'as', 'because', 'since', 'unless' and 'while'. For example, 'I'm tired' and 'I slept well' can be joined together, but the fact that you are tired is more important, so the conjunction you should use is a subordinate conjunction:

> I'm tired _although_ I slept well.

Correlative

Correlative conjunctions come in pairs – they 'correlate', which means that they compare things. They are words such as 'not only … but also', ' either … or' and 'neither … nor', like this:

He is _not only_ annoying _but also_ my brother.
He is _neither_ clever _nor_ funny.
He is _either_ shouting _or_ pinching.
Whether I am alone _or_ with friends he gets on my nerves.

Compound

Lastly, compound conjunctions are made up of more than one word, such as 'so that' or 'as soon as':

> I will stay in my bedroom _as long as_ I like.
> I am hiding _so that_ he won't find me.
> I will come out _as soon as_ they have gone.

OH!

'Oh!' and other words like it are known as interjections, or exclamations. They are words or phrases that appear by themselves with an exclamation mark – often as a warning or to show emotion. You might see them on signs in a safari park or near a school:

> *Elephants!* Please stay in your car.
> *Slow!* Children crossing.

You can use interjections in your own writing to show how someone is feeling – 'Oh yes!', 'Wow!' They can also make great sound effects – 'Pop!', 'Blurrrgh!', 'Wheeeee!' Used well and sparingly, interjections can liven up your writing, but – hey! – do *not* overuse them. Otherwise, people may not pay attention when you use them as commands, as in, 'Go!', 'Help!', 'Listen!' and 'Stop!'

WHICH AM I?

Many words in English can switch from one part of speech to another, depending on how you use them. Here's how:

Switching And Changing

Remember the verbs ending in '-ing'? These letters make up the present participle for all verbs. (See pages 26 to 27 if you'd like a recap.) However, sometimes words that end in '-ing' are actually nouns. They are called 'verbal nouns' because they have been made from a verb. For example:

The *wailing* of the ghost sent shivers down my spine.

Grammar Extra

There are lots of other ways to make nouns from verbs. By adding a different ending, called a 'suffix' (see pages 82 to 87), lots of verbs can be transformed into nouns. For example:

> arrive becomes arriv*al*
> celebrate becomes celebrat*ion*
> inhabit becomes inhabit*ant*

Grammar Guidance. Words that end in '-ing' can also be adjectives, as in:

> The *screaming* fans surrounded the limo.
> The *rising* star hid his face from the crowd.
> The *gabbling* presenter stood in the spotlight.

Preposition Or Adverb?

Many prepositions, such as 'along', 'before', 'behind', 'below', 'down', 'in', 'near', 'on', 'over', 'through' and 'under', can also be adverbs. For example:

> The burglar goes *up* the drainpipe.
> The burglar goes *up*.

In the first sentence, 'up' is a preposition. It tells you what the burglar goes up, which is the drainpipe.

In the second sentence, 'up' is an adverb. It's telling you more about how the burglar goes.

Did You Know?

Some words, such as 'defect' and 'reject', can be verbs or nouns, depending on how you pronounce them (see page 80 for more on this).

BUILDING SENTENCES____

You've probably been building sentences quite happily for years, using all of the parts of speech you have read about here, so here is a quick reminder of the basics.

Nouns And Verbs

When you are writing or speaking, you always need at least two things to make a simple sentence – a noun and a verb. Put a noun and verb together, and you've got a sentence:

> Balloons pop.
> Birds chirp.
> Boys fidget.
> Girls whisper.

The noun is what the sentence is all about – it is known as the subject. 'Balloons', 'birds', 'boys' and 'girls' are all nouns.

The verb provides the action in each sentence. 'Pop', 'chirp', 'fidget' and 'whisper' are all verbs.

What's The Object?

Lots of sentences have an 'object' as well as a subject. The object is also a noun, and it is the part of the sentence that the action is happening to:

> Birds make *nests*.
> Boys guzzle *pizza*.
> Girls stroke *hamsters*.

'Nests', 'pizza' and 'hamsters' are the objects in these three sentences. The nests are being made by the birds, the pizza is being guzzled by the boys, and the hamsters are being stroked by the girls.

Me Or I?

When you're using pronouns in a sentence (see pages 14 to 17), it can be hard to tell if you should use 'me' or 'I', but use this trick and you'll soon work it out:

Imagine your aunt made lunch for you and your brother. Which of these would you say?

>   My aunt made lunch for my brother and *I*.

Or:

>   My aunt made lunch for my brother and *me*.

Leave your brother out to see which sentence works. 'My aunt made lunch for I' sounds wrong, so the second sentence is right. This is because 'aunt' is the subject noun of the sentence – you and your brother are the object nouns, so you use the object form of the pronoun. 'Me' stands in for the object noun and 'I' stands in for the subject noun.

The same trick works in reverse, too. If you and your brother had a go at making lunch instead, which of these would you say?

>   *Me* and my brother made lunch for my aunt.

Or:

>   My brother and *I* made lunch for my aunt.

Get rid of your brother again and you can quickly see that 'Me made lunch for my aunt' makes no sense at all, so the second sentence is correct.

Do You Agree?

The verb in a sentence should always 'agree' with the subject noun. This means choosing the right ending for the verb, so that it matches the noun. For example, boys cannot 'guzzles', they 'guzzle', but a single boy 'guzzles'.

This becomes a bit trickier with collective nouns, such as 'pack' or 'team' (see page 13). Collective nouns can be either singular or plural, so, although there is always more than one member of a team, you can either say, 'The team *is* ready to go,' or, 'The team *are* ready to go.' Just choose either 'is' or 'are' and stick with it.

Building Extensions

Now that you know how a simple sentence is put together, here's how to build even more interesting sentences.

Turning a simple sentence like this:

I threw the ball.

into something like this:

I threw the ball across the garden and it skimmed over the hedge, past the farmyard, then it landed on the horns of an astonished bull.

It's just a matter of building up an idea and adding detail. You can do this by using what are called clauses and phrases (see opposite).

46

_____WHAT'S A CLAUSE?_____

A clause is a group of words within a sentence that has a subject and a verb – just like a sentence. A clause can make sense on its own, but it doesn't have to. For example, these are all clauses from the sentence on the opposite page:

'I threw my ball across the garden'
'it skimmed over the hedge'
'it landed on the horns of
   an astonished bull'.

They each contain a subject and a verb – '*I threw*', '*it skimmed*' and (although this one is trickier to spot), '*it landed* on the horns'.

Who's The Boss?

A sentence can have lots of clauses or just one, but some clauses are more important than others.

A clause that can work on its own as a sentence is called a main clause – it's in charge. A sentence can have two main clauses that are equally important. For example:

I want pizza, and my brother wants pasta.

However, sometimes clauses are not equal. Remember the subordinate conjunctions from page 40? Words such as 'after', 'although', 'as', 'because', 'if', 'since', 'though' and 'unless' are often used to join the main clause to what is called a subordinate clause.

A subordinate clause is one that doesn't make sense on its own – it's not as important as the main clause and doesn't work without one. This sentence has a main clause and a subordinate clause joined together with the word 'although':

I want pizza, although it isn't very healthy.

The words 'it isn't very healthy' don't make much sense alone as you don't know what subject they are talking about – they are a subordinate clause.

Clause Extras

You can use a clause as the subject noun or as the object noun in a sentence. For example:

That I will eat a pizza is certain.

Here, the words 'that I will eat a pizza' act as the object noun of the sentence – this is called a noun clause.

You can also use a clause as an adjective to describe a noun, as in:

The pizza *that has the most toppings* is best.

Here, the words 'that has the most toppings' act as a clause describing the noun 'pizza'.

Lastly, clauses can also act like adverbs, giving more detail to the verb in a sentence:

I ate the pizza *while I watched TV*.

The words 'while I watched TV' give extra detail to how you ate the pizza.

_____WHAT'S A PHRASE?_____

Phrases are groups of words that are useful for adding more interest to the basic idea you are speaking or writing about. They usually don't contain a verb and don't make any sense without the rest of the sentence. For example, the phrase 'left on the plate' doesn't mean anything until you see that:

> There is no pizza
> _left on the plate._

Phrase Extras

A 'noun phrase' is a group of words that acts as an extra-detailed noun. For example:

> _My hungry older sister_ looked at me furiously.

Here, the words 'my hungry older sister' are acting as the subject noun – it's more detailed than just saying 'my sister'.

A phrase can act like an adjective too, as in:

> My sister, _unhappy about her empty plate_, sulked.

Here, the adjective phrase 'unhappy about her empty plate' is a more detailed way of describing your sister.

A phrase can do the job of an adverb too, telling you more about the action going on in the sentence. For example:

> My sister sulked _for as long as she could._

PUTTING THINGS
IN ORDER

Choosing the right words and putting them in the right order can make a lot of difference to your sentences. Even armed with the proper tools for sentence building, it's still possible to make things unclear by accident:

> The stolen treasure was found by a tree.
> I saw three tigers walking round the zoo.

See? Did a tree find some treasure, or was the treasure next to a tree? And what are the chances of three tigers wandering around a zoo unsupervised? Instead, try rewriting the sentences to make more sense. For example:

> The stolen treasure was found beside a tree.
> I was walking round the zoo and saw three tigers.

Action!

There are two ways to use a verb. One is known as the 'active voice', when the subject noun of the sentence is carrying out the action of the verb:

> I smashed the bottle of poison.

The other is the 'passive voice', when the action of the verb happens to the subject noun:

> The bottle of poison was smashed by me.

The passive voice is great for signs in parks and shops:

> Dogs must be kept on a lead.
> All breakages must be paid for.

THE 'WRITE' STYLE

When you're writing a story, you don't need to do lots of explaining right at the start – you can fill in the details later. Instead, grab your readers' attention from the first sentence:

> It was raining hard the day I first met the Itchasnitch witch.

Word Order

Check your word order, too. In long sentences, the most usual order is subject noun, verb, object noun, then another object noun:

> The girl spotted an alien in the kitchen.

You can switch the word order, so that the subject noun (the girl in this case) doesn't come first, but the sentence still makes sense:

> In the kitchen, the girl spotted an alien.

OH, THE ALIEN'S EATEN ALL THE YOGURT AGAIN.

Switching the word order around can make a real difference to how your sentences sound. If your hero is struggling to push a lever and save the world, for instance, which sounds more dramatic? This:

> The lever went down!

or this:

> Down went the lever!

You will also find that it helps to vary your sentence length, as a very short sentence after a few long ones keeps your readers interested. Like this. See? Much better!

Conversation Starters

To make the characters in your story more realistic and more interesting, add some speech. (See pages 106 to 109 for information on speech marks.) A conversation between characters breaks a page of writing into shorter pieces and makes a story much more fun to read:

> "I think I'll have the last biscuit," said Davindra.

> "No, you won't!" Jack replied, stuffing it in his mouth swiftly.

Cutbacks

Lastly, look back at what you've written. Are there any words in there you don't need or that don't add anything? If so, take them out.

Look especially hard at how many adverbs you are using. You might, for example, say:

> he said, grumpily
> he said, excitedly.

Think about whether the adverbs really add anything though. Could you show that he was grumpy or excited with the words that your character says instead?

_____TEACHER STUNNING_____

Here is a quick checklist of some useful grammatical terms. Throw these casually into conversation with your teachers and watch them fall to the classroom floor, stunned by your genius!

Allegory

An allegory is a story that seems to be about one subject, but actually has a hidden meaning. It can give a message or symbolize a moral.

Alliteration

Are you a budding poet? If so, alliteration is for you. It is when you repeat a letter, usually at the start of a word, to create a feeling or an effect, or to create atmosphere:

> … the low last edge of the long lone land.

Assonance

Assonance is similar to alliteration, but uses repeating vowel sounds to create an interesting effect, like this:

> What noise annoys an oyster most?

Assonance can also be the repetition of consonants, for example, in the words, 'wash', 'wish' and 'whoosh'.

Rappers use alliteration and assonance all the time, and so do adverts – so listen out next time you're watching TV.

Clichés

A cliché is an expression that is so overused that everyone is bored with it – you probably hear these all the time:

> It's raining cats and dogs.
> Quick as a flash.

Hyperbole

When you are speaking or writing, you might deliberately exaggerate what you are saying to create an effect. This is called hyperbole (pronounced 'high-per-boh-lee'). It is a million, billion times more effective if you use it sparingly!

Metaphors

Metaphors describe a person or thing as *being* something else – they compare things for effect, but aren't really true. For example:

> She's a real dragon.
> You're a pain in the neck.

Oxymorons

An oxymoron combines two things that contradict each other, for example:

> a definite maybe
> silent applause
> an open secret.

Paradox

A paradox is a statement that contradicts itself. For example, someone might say, "I always bend the truth," but are they telling the truth or lying when they say that?

Personification

If you are writing a story, you might give human characteristics to an animal or even an object. This is called personification.

Similes

A simile is used to compare one person or thing to another – they're easy to spot as they often use the words 'like' or 'as', as in:

> as cold as ice
> run like the wind.

Synonyms And Antonyms

Synonyms are words with similar meanings. The words 'enormous', 'immense' and 'vast' can all describe something 'huge'. Using synonyms is a good way to avoid repeating yourself and a thesaurus is full of them (see page 23).

Antonyms are words that have opposite meanings – 'big' and 'small' or 'hot' and 'cold', for example.

Tautology

Tautology is the repetition of words with the same meaning, such as a 'free gift', a 'short summary' and 'very unique'. It is best avoided.

BAD GRAMMAR!

Years ago, it was bad grammar to 'split' an infinitive – by putting another word between 'to' and the verb. For example:

I am going to quickly eat something before ballet.

It was also bad grammar to put a preposition at the end of a sentence:

What are you talking about?

Now the rules are more relaxed. Many people do use split infinitives, and do put prepositions at the ends of sentences. Languages develop all the time – people create new words and phrases, such as 'docusoap', 'email' and 'fashion-victim', every day. People even find new uses for old words – people 'tweet' on the Internet, and computer screens have 'wallpaper'.

And Finally ...

Just as language moves on, so does grammar, but one thing that doesn't change is the richness of the English language. So use it well!

SPELLING THINGS OUT___

In some countries, spelling is a simple business. There are rules about how different sounds should be spelled and all the words obey them. However, English isn't like that. For example, the word 'weight' rhymes with 'ate', but almost all the letters are different. Confusing, isn't it?

A Language Invasion

Over the centuries, Britain has been invaded by people from many countries and each of them brought their own language with them. Many words and spellings were adopted from foreign languages and adapted into English.

The Romans brought Latin with them, so many English words come from Latin, including 'alien', 'unicorn', 'ignite', 'pavement', 'animal' and 'agenda'. The Vikings from Scandinavia brought Norse words – 'anger', 'blackmail', 'ugly', 'cake', 'freckle' and 'wand' all come from Norse. Many words, including 'romance', 'castle', 'royal' and 'blue' come from French, which was spoken by Norman invaders.

Word Swipers

As if that wasn't enough, the English language has often pinched words from other countries, too, such as 'pyjamas' and 'jodhpurs' from India, 'canoe' from the Caribbean, and 'anorak' from Inuktitut – the Inuit languages spoken in the north of Canada.

To help with all these different spellings you can look things up in a dictionary, and that is always the best way to be sure of how to spell words (see pages 69 to 70 for more on dictionaries). However, over the following pages you will find seriously helpful advice to help you sort out how to spell all kinds of individual words and groups of words.

Read on to discover how you can become a whizz at spelling to help make your writing the best it can be.

SOUNDS ODD

One of the strangest things about English spelling is that although most of the time you can work out how a word is spelled by saying it out loud, this doesn't always work. In fact, more than ten per cent of the words used in the English language are not spelled the way they sound! Some of them are words you just have to learn, but there are lots of useful rules to help you, too.

Tools Of The Trade

If you're reading this, you've obviously got to grips with the number-one tool of the trade: the alphabet. You know that it has 26 letters and that five are vowels – **a**, **e**, **i**, **o** and **u** – and the rest are consonants ... or are they?

The letter **y** is counted as a consonant, but it's also a part-time vowel. At the beginning of a word, such as 'yes' or 'yacht', it acts as a consonant; at the end of a word, such as 'happy' or 'silly', it acts as a vowel. In the case of the word 'rhythm', it's definitely a vowel.

Added Extras

Spelling Extra. Throughout this section, you'll find 'Spelling Extras' that give you extra information about the spelling rules you've just read about.

Spelling Specials. These will give you useful tips to help you put the spelling rules to good use.

Did You Know? Each 'Did You Know?' heading will introduce an extra spelling fact that you're sure to enjoy.

VITAL VOWELS

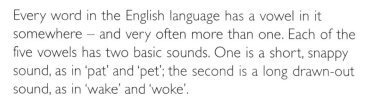

Every word in the English language has a vowel in it somewhere – and very often more than one. Each of the five vowels has two basic sounds. One is a short, snappy sound, as in 'pat' and 'pet'; the second is a long drawn-out sound, as in 'wake' and 'woke'.

The long vowel sound is spelled with what is sometimes known as the 'magic **e**', so that:

> hat becomes hate
> pet becomes Pete (short for 'Peter')
> fin becomes fine
> rob becomes robe
> cub becomes cube.

Spelling Special. There are some exceptions to the rule, including the words 'have', 'give' and 'love', which are not pronounced with the long vowel.

Spelling Extra

The magic **e** is also known as a 'split digraph' because the vowels are separated, or split, by a consonant, but that doesn't sound as much fun, does it?

Syllables

Each part of a word with a vowel sound in it is called a 'syllable'. The word 'ban' has one syllable; the word 'banana' has three: *'ba-na-na'.*

I Before E

Here's a well-known spelling tip you're sure to come across:

I before **e**, except after **c**,
Or when sounded like **a**
As in neighbour and weigh.

This means that, as a general rule, **e** should follow **i** in words such as 'piece', 'believe' and 'field' unless there is a letter **c** before it, as in 'receipt' and 'receive'.

There are, however, some sneaky exceptions to this rule such as 'weird', which also makes the long **e** sound.

Spelling Special. The letter **q** goes nowhere alone – it's always got a **u** next to it, as in 'quiz' and 'question'. Even in the middle or near the end of a word, as in 'require' or 'cheque', **q** sticks with its **u**.

Did You Know?

'Diphthong' is a funny word for sounds you make all the time, for instance in the words 'feel' and 'fail'. The vowel sound changes as you say the word aloud because your tongue moves from one position to another in one syllable.

Vowel Tips

As well as the two basic vowel sounds, it is possible to combine different letters to make other sounds, too. For example the 'aw' sound in 'four' is made with the letters **o**, **u** and **r**. Use the list opposite to spot the different ways these sounds can be spelled.

Vowel Checker

In the list below, each vowel sound has examples of the ways the sound can be spelled, with the different letters highlighted in **bold**.

A

A short 'a' sound, as in 'hat':

cat
pl**ai**t.

A long 'a' sound, as in 'hate':

pl**a**te
m**ai**d
l**ay**
br**ea**k
eight
gr**ey**
g**au**ge.

An 'ah' sound, as in 'pass':

v**a**se
ah
h**a**lf
arm
l**au**gh.

An 'air' sound, as in 'fair':

h**air**
sp**are**
y**eah**
p**ear**
th**eir**
wh**ere**.

An 'aw' sound, as in 'dawn':

f**a**ll
t**a**lk
c**augh**t
sp**aw**n
r**oar**
d**oor**
sp**or**t
th**ough**t
f**our**
s**ure**.

E

A short 'e' sound, as in 'pet':

y**e**t
d**ea**d
fri**e**nd.

A long 'e' sound, as in 'Pete':

qu**ay**
eke
fl**ea**
fl**ee**
dec**ei**ve
k**ey**
f**ie**ld
sard**i**ne.

An 'ear' sound, as in 'hear':

f**ear**
ch**eer**
h**ere**
t**ier**.

An 'er' sound, as in 'her':

l**ear**n
j**er**k
b**ir**d
w**or**d
j**our**ney
c**ur**d.

I

A short 'i' sound, as in 'fin':

bin
build
mystery.

A long 'i' sound, as in 'fine':

lime
tie
sigh
dry
goodbye.

O

A short 'o' sound, as in 'rob':

wasp
sausage
spot
trough.

A long 'o' sound, as in 'robe':

hope
soap
foe
glow.

An 'ow' sound, as in 'clown':

allow
pound.

An 'oy' sound, as in 'toy':

annoy
coin
buoy.

U

A short 'u' sound, as in 'cub':

come
young
pun.

A long 'u' sound, as in 'cube' (which sounds like 'you'):

stew
duty
Tuesday.

A 'u' sound, as in 'flute':

do
root
soup
plume
true
fruit.

A 'u' sound, as in 'bush':

look
could
full.

COOL CONSONANTS

Consonants are all the letters of the alphabet that aren't vowels – except the letter **y**, which sometimes behaves like a vowel and sometimes acts like a consonant (see page 60).

Consonants can work alone, in pairs and even in groups. For example, the letters **n**, **g**, **t**, **h** and **s** don't look as though they could make any sense together, but put them in the word 'strengths' and they do. ('Strengths' is the longest word in the English language with just one vowel.)

Consonant Checker

Some consonant sounds can be spelled in more than one way. See how each of the sounds can be written below.

F as in 'four':

> friend
> gaffe
> cough
> photo.

G as in 'great':

> go
> egg
> ghoul
> guess.

J as in 'jellies':

> jolly
> edge
> gigantic.

K as in 'kites':

> kick
> count
> account
> echo
> block
> bouquet
> plaque.

S as in 'sooner':

> said
> nice
> science
> kiss.

'Sh' as in 'shoes':

> shopping
> machine
> social
> sugar
> tension
> assure
> possession
> mention.

Y as in 'yapping':

> you
> use.

Z as in 'zoo':

> zip
> daisy.

65

Soft, Soft, Soft

The letters **c** and **g** both have two different sounds – one hard, as in the words 'cold' and 'gold'; one soft, as in 'cell' and 'gel'. The letters **c** and **g** are usually soft whenever they are followed by the letter **e**, **i**, or **y**. For example:

> sau*c*er and *g*erm
> de*c*ide and *g*iant
> *g*ymnast and *c*ylinder.

Some words, such as 'circus' and 'garage', even have both the hard and the soft sounds in them.

Consonants And Suffixes

Adding a new ending to a word is known as adding a 'suffix' (see pages 82 to 87). You sometimes need to double the consonant at the end of the word. This happens when:

- the word has one syllable
- the word ends in a single consonant following a vowel
- the suffix – or word ending – begins with a vowel.

For example:

> flat becomes fla*tter*
> nod becomes no*dding*
> tap becomes ta*pped*.

Doubling the consonant makes sure that the vowel sound stays the same when you add your suffix. This is easy enough in short, one-syllable words, but in longer words you need to listen to how they are pronounced to decide whether you need to double the consonant or not.

When you say a long word aloud, usually you stress, or 'emphasize', a particular part of the word. For example, when you say the word 'enter', you stress the first syllable, but when you say the word 'prefer', you stress the second syllable. This means that when you are adding a suffix, you need to double the letter **r** at the end of the word 'prefer', but you don't need to double it at the end of 'enter':

> enter becomes ente*red* and ente*ring*
> prefer becomes prefe*rred* and prefe*rring*.

Spelling Special. Words that end in the letter **l** after a single vowel do not follow this rule. You must always double the letter **l** when adding an extra ending to words such as 'travel' and 'pedal':

> travel becomes trave*lled* and trave*ller*
> pedal becomes peda*lled* and peda*lling*.

See pages 85 to 86 for more on l-endings.

SNEAKY SPELLINGS

Some spellings are extra sneaky. Words that contain the 'ough' spelling can make all these different sounds:

cough, which rhymes with 'off'
bough, which rhymes with 'ow'
thorough, which rhymes with 'uh'
though, which rhymes with 'oh'
thought, which rhymes with 'aw'
through, which rhymes with 'ooh'
tough, which rhymes with 'uff'.

Not so long ago, it was even used to make an 'up' sound, when spelling 'hiccough', but now the spelling 'hiccup' has almost replaced it. Much more sensible.

One-And-Only Words

Some spellings are one-offs – words you just have to learn because there's no way of guessing how to spell them from their sound. Here are three to begin with:

beauty
biscuit
moustache.

Did You Know?

The famous scientist Albert Einstein, who developed theories about time and space, was a genius, but even he found spelling quite tricky.

___DICTIONARY DETECTIVES___

It's important to get to know how to use a dictionary, whether it's to check your spelling or to look up the meaning of a word you're stuck on.

Know Your ABCs

Once you know the order of the alphabet, you're well on your way to being able to use a dictionary because that's how dictionaries are organized. Words beginning with **a** are followed by words beginning with **b**, which are followed by words beginning with **c** and so on.

What happens if two words begin with the same letter though? Would you find 'type' before or after 'tape'?

If two words begin with the same letter, the dictionary uses the second letters to put them in order. Whichever comes first in the alphabet, comes first in the dictionary:

tape comes before type.

If the second letters are the same, the third letter is used to sort them out: so 'tame' comes before 'tape'. This goes on until a letter that's different crops up, for example:

truce comes before truck.

No Trouble

If you haven't got a clue how to spell a word – 'trouble', for example – try saying it aloud. You might guess quite closely with 'trubble' or 'trubbel', but you might guess something like 'chrubble'. When a word is nowhere to be seen in your dictionary, try asking yourself these questions:

- What sound can I hear at the start of the word?
- Am I sure I've got it right with 'chr'?
- What other ways could that sound be spelled?

You can also use the Consonant Checker list on page 65 to narrow down what the first letter might be. Once you've worked out the beginning of a word, use the Vowel Checker list to help you spell the next sound (see pages 63 and 64).

Silent Letters

Occasionally, you might find that you have a spot of bother working out the first letter of a word because … *shhh!* … it's silent! Here are some examples that you're likely to come across quite often:

> **g** as in gnash, gnat and
>   gnome
> **h** as in honest, hour and heir
> **k** as in knee, knob,
>   knot and knife
> **p** as in psychology, pneumonia
>   and pterodactyl
> **w** as in who, whole,
>   wrong and write.

Spelling Special. Lots of silent letters always come hand in hand with a particular letter or letters.

For instance, a silent **k** is only ever before the letter **n**; a silent **p** is always before **n**, **s** or **t**; a silent **w** is always before the letters **h** or **r**.

More Silent Letters

There are also words that have a silent letter in the middle or at the end. Even though you can't hear them you still need to write them out. Here are some of the most common ones to watch out for:

b as in comb, lamb, thumb, debt and subtle

g as in design, resign and sign

h as in rhinoceros, rhubarb, rhyme, what, when, where, whip, white and why

l as in calm, half, talk and walk

n as in autumn, condemn, hymn and solemn

s as in aisle and island

t as in castle, listen, rustle and whistle

w as in sword and answer.

Spelling Special. The letter **e** on the end of words usually isn't pronounced – for example, as in 'tape' and 'hope'.

Did You Know?

Silent letters weren't always silent. Until Shakespeare's time, for example, the **k** in 'knight' was still sounded out. Gradually, the way these words are said has changed, but the spellings have stayed the same.

SPELLING PLURALS

A singular noun tells you there's just one of something – an 'apple' or a 'cat', for instance. Plurals are nouns that tell you there is more than one of something, as in 'apples' and 'cats'.

Plural Endings

Most of the time, you make a plural by adding a letter **s** to the end of a word. However, there are lots of words where this doesn't work – just try to say 'witchs' or 'wishs' and you'll see why. For words that end in '-ch', '-sh', '-ss', '-tch', '-x' or '-z' you'll need to use '-es' instead of just '-s' to make the plural. 'Witches' and 'wishes' are much easier to say!

Here are some other examples:

arch becomes arches
bush becomes bushes
pass becomes passes
watch becomes watches
fox becomes foxes
klutz becomes klutzes.

Plurals Checklist

Y-Endings. If the letter before the **y** is a vowel, as in 'day', put an **s** on the end:

day becomes days.

If the letter before the **y** is a consonant, as in 'lolly', drop the **y** and add '-ies', so:

lolly becomes lollies.

The only time you don't do that is with names, as they always stay the same:

The Kennedy family lives next door.
The Kennedys live next door.

F-Endings. If a word ends in two **f**s, as in 'cliff', you simply add an **s** to make 'cliffs'. However, for words that end in a single letter **f**, or the letters **f** and **e**, you need to drop the **f** and change the ending to '-ves' to make the plural, as in:

elf becomes elves
knife becomes knives
leaf becomes leaves
life becomes lives.

Spelling Special. There are a few exceptions to the **f**-ending rule – these words don't take the '-ves' ending when you make the plural:

belief becomes beliefs
chief becomes chiefs
roof becomes roofs.

O-Endings. Unfortunately, there's no fixed rule for words that end in the letter **o**. Their plurals either end in just '-s' or '-es'. It's worth learning these:

buffaloes
dominoes
echoes
heroes
mosquitoes
potatoes
tomatoes.

Weird Plurals.
Some words are quite different when they become plurals. These are worth remembering:

child becomes children
mouse becomes mice
goose becomes geese.

Plurals Of Hyphenated Words. Some nouns are made up of two or more words joined by hyphens. These are called hyphenated nouns. Most of the time you can simply pop an **s** on the last word to make the plural, but there are some exceptions. For example, in the word 'sister-in-law' sister is more important than law, so it becomes 'sisters-in-law'.

When In Rome. Remember how a lot of English words came from Roman invaders? Well, they left their Latin plurals here, too, and some words still work happily with Latin endings as well as with '-s' endings. Latin word endings work like this:

- -a changes to -ae, so antenna becomes antennae*
- -is changes to -es, so axis becomes axes
- -us changes to -i, so hippopotamus becomes hippopotami*
- -um changes to -a, so medium becomes media.

Did You Know?

Some words, such as 'deer', 'moose' and 'sheep', stay the same – whether you have one sheep or a whole flock of sheep. The plural of 'fish' can be 'fishes' or just 'fish', but some words, such as 'trousers', are only ever plural and don't have a singular at all. These include:

>clothes
>glasses (that you see through)
>pants (as in underwear)
>scissors
>shorts (that you wear).

* However, 'antennas' and 'hippopotamuses' are also accepted ways of spelling these two words.

NEW BEGINNINGS!

You can add to the beginning of a word using what's known as a prefix. This is a letter or group of letters that change the meaning of the main word. 'Pre-' itself means 'before' or 'in front', which might help to remind you what a prefix is.

Prefix Checklist

You can often work out the meaning of a word that has a prefix bolted on to it if you have an idea of what the prefix means. Here are some you'll come across a lot, with some examples of words that they appear in:

ab-	away, from	*ab*sent and *ab*stract
ad-	towards	*ad*vance and *ad*vantage
anti-	against, opposing	*anti*clockwise and *anti*septic
de-	from, out, down	*de*part and *de*scend
ex-	out of, away from	*ex*it and *ex*tract
extra-	outside, beyond	*extra*ordinary
inter-	between, among	*inter*national and *inter*view
intra-	within, inside	*intra*venous
mal-	bad, wrong	*mal*ign and *mal*practice
re-	back, again	*re*do and *re*appear
semi-	half	*semi*circle
sub-	below, under	*sub*marine and *sub*standard
tele-	far off	*tele*scope and *tele*port.

Topsy-Turvy

Prefixes, such as 'dis-', 'il-', 'im-', 'in-', 'ir-', 'mis-' and 'un-', change words so completely that they give them the opposite meaning, so that:

> obey becomes *dis*obey
> logical becomes *il*logical
> possible becomes *im*possible
> attentive becomes *in*attentive
> regular becomes *ir*regular
> behave becomes *mis*behave
> interesting becomes *un*interesting.

Spelling Special. The main word and the prefix always keep all their letters, even if two of the same letters end up joined together as in 'natural' and 'unnatural'. (Plus, of course, 'spell' and 'misspell'!)

Extra-Special

Some prefixes, such as 'super-', add to the meaning of a word, so that a 'hero' becomes a 'superhero'. Super comes from a Latin word meaning 'above', so a superhero is better than a normal hero.

SOUNDS LIKE ...

There are quite a few words in English that sound alike, but that aren't spelled the same and have different meanings. For example, 'knot' and 'not', and 'whole' and 'hole'.

These words, and others like them, are known as homophones. Here are some of the ones you're most likely to come across:

allowed and aloud	read and reed
beach and beech	right and write
boy and buoy	sail and sale
fair and fare	their and there
hear and here	too and two
know and no	wear and where
pale and pail	weather and whether
passed and past	which and witch
plain and plane	wood and would.

Spelling Special. In words such as 'it's' and 'its', and 'who's' and 'whose', apostrophes can cause a homophone headache. Turn to page 117 to find out more about them.

Boing! Boing!

There's a whole group of words that try to get as close to a real-life sound as they can. The words 'sizzle', 'slap', 'slurp', 'smash', 'snap', 'splutter', 'swish' and 'swoosh' are all using what is called onomatopoeia (pronounced 'on-uh-mat-oh-pee-ya'). This is when words spell out the way that something sounds.

Things 'click' and things 'crackle', things go 'kerplunk' and 'kerching'. Horses 'clip-clop' and clocks 'tick-tock'. Corks 'pop', cars 'vroom' and rockets 'zoom'. Children who catch colds go 'atishoo!' and toddlers who fall go 'boo-hoo'.

Then there are animal noises too:

buzz
heehaw
miaow
oink
quack
squawk
squeak
twitter
woof.

Heteronyms

These are words that are spelled the same, have different meanings and that are also pronounced differently. For example, 'does', when it rhymes with 'buzz', is part of the verb 'to do', but when it rhymes with 'froze' it means more than one female deer!

Homographs

These are words which are spelled the same, but that have different meanings. For example:

I gave friend a *present*.
I had to *present* my project to the class.

The film left a *tear* in my eye.
I couldn't *tear* myself away.

The *wind* blew the washing away.
I helped my granny to *wind* her wool.

Spelling Special. Sometimes homographs are pronounced differently when they have different meanings. For example, a '*rebel*' – with the stress at the beginning of the word – is a person who '*rebels*'; 'to re*bel*', with the stress at the end of the word, is a verb meaning to disobey the rules. You need to read the sentence that words like these appear in to decide which meaning is meant and which way it should be said.

Did You Know?

Other languages use onomatopoeia, too. English cats may 'purr', but French cats go 'ron-ron'; and German cats go 'schnurr'.

Invent-A-Word

You can have a lot of fun with onomatopoeia, inventing new words for any kind of sound. The beauty of it is this: you can be as adventurous with your spelling as you like – and no one can tell you it's wrong.

What noise does a toaster make when it pops up? 'Pdung', maybe? Or how about the sound of nails scraped down a blackboard? 'Skrercccch'? And how would you spell the sound of water going down a plughole?

GOOD ADVICE

Some words, such as 'practice' and 'practise', are easy to muddle as they sound the same or very similar. With a **c** it is a noun (practice) and with an **s** it is a verb (practise) – remember that the letter **c** comes before the letter **s** in the alphabet and that the word 'noun' comes before the word 'verb' in the alphabet, too.

Which One?

Another easy way to remember this rule is to remind yourself that the words 'advice' and 'advise' follow the same rule, but sound different. Try to put them in a sentence:

I *practiced* all day.
I *practised* all day.

If you can't decide which is right, try the sentence with 'advice' and 'advise' instead:

I *adviced* all day.
I *advised* all day.

ADVISE **ADVICE**
ADVISE **ADVICE**
ADVISE **ADVICE**
ADVISE **ADVICE**
ADVISE **ADVICE**

Now it's easier to tell that 'I practised all day' is correct.

Quite a few other words are easy to confuse, but putting them in a sentence often helps. Try these two:

I accept your invitation.
Everyone was invited except me.

'Accept' means to take something or say 'yes' – if you were invited to a party, for example. 'Except' means to leave out.

STICKY ENDINGS

A 'suffix' is a word ending, such as '-ed', which makes the past tense, and '-ly', which often makes an adverb. A suffix is added to a word to make the word work in a different way. For example, the suffixes '-hood', '-ish' and '-like' can be added to 'child' to make 'childhood', 'childish' and 'childlike'.

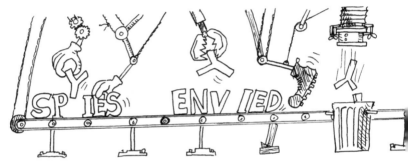

No End Of Suffixes

There are lots and lots of suffixes you're sure to come across. Many words, just like 'child', can happily use different endings to change their meaning.

There's cap*able*, compli*ance*, pleas*ant*, comment*ary*, hibern*ation*, pati*ence*, independ*ent*, bake*ry*, hope*ful*, beauti*fully*, horr*ible*, wish*ing*, ar*ise*, self*ish*, hero*ism*, speech*less*, life*like*, love*ly*, amuse*ment*, strange*ness*, direct*ory*, danger*ous*, proced*ure* and many, many more!

Suffixes Checklist

E-Endings. For words that end with the letter **e**, take a look at the suffix – if it begins with a vowel, as in '-ation', '-ing' and '-ism', drop the **e** then add the suffix. For example:

imagine (imagin -ation) imagination
pounce (pounc -ing) pouncing
favourite (favourit -ism) favouritism.

However, if you are adding the suffix '-ing' to a word ending in the letters '-ie', as in 'lie' and 'tie', replace those letters with the letter **y** before tacking on '-ing'. Otherwise you'll get 'liing' and 'tiing' instead of 'lying' and 'tying'!

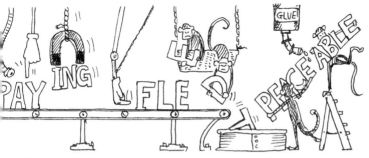

Y Special. For words that end in the letter **y** (the part-time vowel) the rule can vary. If the letter before the **y** is a consonant, as in 'envy' and 'sticky', replace the **y** with an **i**:

envy becomes envied and enviable
sticky becomes stickier and stickiest.

If the suffix starts with the letter **i**, as in '-ing', keep the **y**:

envy and envying.

You also need to keep the **y** if the letter before it is a vowel:

pay and paying
annoy and annoyance.

Spelling Special. One-syllable words that end in **y**, such as 'spy' and 'cry', have their own rule. Keep the **y**-ending unless you are adding the suffixes '-ed' or '-es':

> spy becomes spied or spies
> cry becomes cried or cries.

The letter **y** can be a suffix all by itself when it is making words such as 'pimply' and 'simply'. In these sorts of words the part-time vowel takes the same rule as other suffixes starting with a vowel – drop the **e** and add the suffix '-y':

> pimple (pimpl -y) pimply.

Rule-Breakers

For words that end in two **e**s, an **o** and an **e** or a **y** and an **e**, you need to keep the letter **e** when you are adding a suffix. For example:

> flee becomes fleeing and flees
> eye becomes eyeing and eyes
> toe becomes toeing and toes.

Even the rule-breaker has a rule-breaker though. If you are adding the suffix '-ed', remove the letter **e** so that:

> flee becomes fled
> eye becomes eyed
> toe becomes toed.

For words such as 'peace', 'singe' and 'outrage' you must keep the letter **e**, or the **c** and **g** sounds become hard instead of soft. So:

> peace becomes peaceable
> singe becomes singeing
> outrage becomes outrageous.

Spelling Special. Keep the **e** in words such as 'dye' so that you don't muddle 'dyeing' and 'dying'!

Odd Ones Out. When you are adding the suffix '-ous', there are some words where you need to take out the **e** even if it isn't at the end of the word. These include the words 'disaster', 'monster' and 'wonder'. So:

> disaster becomes disastrous,
>   not distasterous
> monster becomes monstrous,
>   not monsterous
> wonder becomes wondrous,
>   not wonderous.

L-Words. For words that end in the letter **l**, count the number of vowels that come together just before it. If there's a single vowel, as in 'travel' for example, double the **l** before adding a suffix:

> travelled and travelling.

If there are two vowels, as in 'wheel', don't double the **l**:

> wheeled and wheeling.

When you are describing something as 'full' – full of joy or full of care, for instance – add the suffix '-ful' to the word, but make sure you drop the last **l**:

> joy and full becomes joyful
> care and full becomes careful.

85

However, when you add the suffix '-fully' to a word, make sure that you keep the double l. For example:

joyfully and carefully.

Spelling Special. You need to drop a letter l from the word 'skill' to make 'skilful' and 'skilfully'.

Other Doubles. If the main word has one syllable and the suffix begins with a vowel, double the consonant. So:

dig becomes digging
hot becomes hotter.

For longer words, say the word aloud and listen to where you stress the word. If you stress the first syllable, as in 'enter', you don't double the consonant. If you stress the second syllable, as in 'admit' and 'begin', you do double:

admit becomes admitting
begin becomes beginning.

If the word ends in two vowels before a consonant or if it ends in two consonants you don't need to double:

peel becomes peeling
stick becomes sticking.

Poss*ible* Or Poss*able*? The suffixes '-able' and '-ible' sound similar, but there are ways to tell them apart. The suffix '-able' often has a hard-sounding **c** or **g** before it, as in:

applicable and huggable.

The suffix '-ible' often has a soft-sounding **c** or **g** or a hissing **s** sound in front of it, as in:

legible and possible.

What's The Difference? The suffixes '-ance' and '-ence' can turn verbs into nouns. For example, 'difference' from 'differ'. Verbs that end with the emphasis on a single vowel followed by **r** always use the suffix '-ence' to make a noun:

occur becomes occurrence
prefer becomes preference.

Is It Important? Words ending in '-ant' and '-ent' are often adjectives. They match their nouns, so it's:

abundant and abundance
entrant and entrance
different and difference
excellent and excellence.

Stationary Or Stationery? Don't muddle 'stationary', which means not moving, with 'stationery', which means things like pens, paper and envelopes. Remember that 'station*ery*' has a letter **e** in it, just like the words 'p*e*n' and '*e*nvelope'.

Did You Know?

'Supersede' is the only word that ends in '-sede' – all the other words that end in the same sound, such as 'precede' and 'proceed', are spelled '-cede' or '-ceed'.

SPELLING MUDDLER

Once you've got the hang of spelling, there are some brilliant ways to mess around with the English language.

Anagrams

An anagram is where you take the letters of one word or a group of words, and turn them into something different. For instance, the word 'carthorse' has the same letters as the word 'orchestra'.

The best anagrams make a related word or phrase (sort of!) from the letters of the first word or words, like these:

> schoolmaster – the classroom
> the Morse Code – here come dots
> William Shakespeare – I am a weakish speller.

Why not try it yourself?

Palindromes

You could also try 'palindromes' – words that are spelled the same way forwards and backwards. 'Eye', 'deed', 'level', 'noon', 'pip', 'pop' and 'toot' are all palindromes. You can make them from whole sentences, too. For example:

> Don't nod.
> Was it Eliot's toilet I saw?
> Never odd or even.

Did You Know?

A man named William Archibald Spooner was known for accidentally switching the beginnings of words around as he spoke. These mistakes became known as 'spoonerisms'. For example, if you mean to say, 'Stop flipping the channel!' but instead say, 'Stop chipping the flannel!' this is a spoonerism. It can happen all the time, especially if you are in a rush, or nervous, like William Spooner.

> a crushing blow – a blushing crow
> a pack of lies – a lack of pies
> it's pouring with rain – it's roaring with pain
> you have bad manners – you have mad banners
> a half-formed wish – a half-warmed fish
> lighting a fire – fighting a liar
> blow your nose – know your blows
> save the whales – wave the sails.

And Finally ...

A great way to get the hang of spelling is to read and read and read. You can read anything, not just books – the backs of cereal packets, comics, gaming instructions, your sister's secret diary (okay, maybe not that one). It all helps.

The more you read, the more spellings sneak their way into your brain. So have fun with spelling – and get reading!

LET'S GO!

Take a look at these paragraphs. Which one do you think is using the right punctuation?

This one:

> The house looked deserted. Empty. I pushed open the door. "Hello," I called. Silence. No one answered. Just then, I heard a noise. Crrrrrrk. A floorboard. Then … footsteps!

Or this one:

> The house looked deserted, empty. I pushed open the door. "Hello?" I called. Silence: no one answered. Just then, I heard a noise – *crrrrrrk* – a floorboard. Then footsteps.

Actually, they both are. This is because, although there are rules you need to learn, punctuation does give you options, so there's no need for apostrophe panic or hyphen horrors!

The important thing is to use punctuation to make your writing clear. The marks you use give extra information about your writing, like leaving a trail of clues for your reader. They help to show exactly what you mean.

Added Extras

Punctuation Extra. Throughout this section, you'll find 'Punctuation Extras' that give you extra information about the spelling rules you've just read about.

Punctuation Pointer. These will give you useful tips to help you put the punctuation rules to good use.

Did You Know? You'll find an extra punctuation fact you're sure to enjoy under each 'Did You Know?' heading.

A Trail Of Clues

When you speak, you give lots of clues to help people understand what you're saying. You raise and lower your voice; you leave long and short pauses; you use gestures – all to help another person understand what you are saying. That's what punctuation does when you are writing.

A simple change of punctuation mark can convey a lot of things about your tone of voice, too. Suppose a friend looked at your outfit for an important occasion, and gushed:

"That's your best outfit ever!"

You'd be pleased, confident, ready to go – but if he or she looked at your outfit and said, in a questioning tone:

"That's your best outfit ever?"

You'd probably get changed! One little mark on the page can have the same effect. That is the magic of punctuation.

FULL STOPS

A full stop might not be much to look at, but don't be fooled. It does a huge amount for such a small dot. The most important thing a full stop does is to tell you when a sentence is finished, otherwise this happens:

> It was a bright sunny day there wasn't a cloud in the sky in just a few hours I'd be on a train in a few more hours I'd be putting up the tent with Dad we had a whole week of camping ahead

Try reading it aloud. It's hard, isn't it? Everything's confused. None of it makes sense and you run out of breath. If you put in some full stops it's a completely different matter:

> It was a bright sunny day. There wasn't a cloud in the sky. In just a few hours I'd be on a train. In a few more hours I'd be putting up the tent with Dad. We had a whole week of camping ahead.

The full stops tell you where to pause. They give you time to take in the meaning of a sentence and gather your breath before reading the next sentence.

Punctuation Pointer. Sentences always start with a capital letter. See pages 122 to 124 for more on capitals.

Abbreviations

Full stops can be used for jobs other than ending sentences. When you shorten a word, it's called an abbreviation – such as 'Mon.' for 'Monday' or 'Tues.' for 'Tuesday'. The full stop at the end shows that the word has been shortened. However, it is becoming more and more usual not to bother with the full stop.

There are times though when it's a good idea to use full stops to make things clear. Here are two you will often use:

> I went to bed at 9 p.m. last night.
> I got up at 7 a.m. this morning.

When an abbreviation could be confused with another word – 'a.m.' and 'am', for example – it's important to make things as clear as possible.

Did You Know?

The abbreviations a.m. and p.m. come from the Latin words *ante meridiem* (before midday) and *post meridiem* (after midday). Use full stops for both of them.

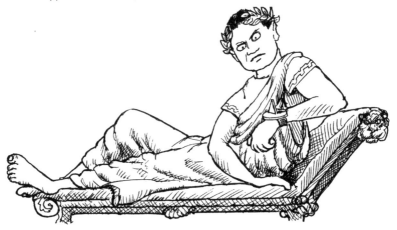

Contractions

Contractions are words that are shortened by keeping the beginning and end, but taking out the middle:

> Dr is short for doctor
> Mr is short for Mister
> Mrs is short for Mistress (pronounced 'missus') …

In the past, people used full stops at the end of these words to show they had shortened the word, but now it isn't necessary and can even seem old-fashioned.

You may also see this kind of abbreviation quite often – 'no.' – it is a 'contraction' that comes from the Latin word *numero*, meaning number. In this case, you need to use the full stop to make it clear that you don't mean the word 'no':

> Rule no. 1: no midnight feasts.
> Rule no. 2: no jumping on furniture.

Punctuation Pointer. If your sentence ends with an abbreviation you don't need to add an extra full stop. So it wouldn't be:

> I went to bed at 9 p.m..

It would be:

> I went to bed at 9 p.m.

Don't Stop These

An 'acronym' is a word that is formed from, or based on, the initial letters or syllables of a group of words (see page 61 for more on syllables). You don't need to put full stops between each letter.

Lots of acronyms use capital letters:

> POW – Prisoner Of War
> UFO – Unidentified Flying Object
> USA – United States of America

Some acronyms don't use capital letters and are used as nouns. For instance, a **l**ight **a**mplification by **s**timulated **e**mission of **r**adiation is actually a 'laser'; **ra**dio **d**etection **a**nd **r**anging is called 'radar'; a **s**elf-**c**ontained **u**nderwater **b**reathing **a**pparatus is usually known as a 'scuba'.

_____OTHER STOPS_____

There are two more ways to end a sentence apart from a full stop. A question mark (**?**) or an exclamation mark (**!**) can go in place of a full stop, like this:

> Are you coming to the park?
> Let's go on the swings!

Is That A Question?

Sentences which are questions are usually shown with a question mark at the end of them. Spotting when you need to use a question mark is easy when the sentence uses a 'question word' like these:

> How? What? When? Where? Who? Why?

Or when it is a longer, 'direct question', like these:

> How did you do that back flip?
> What made you think you could eat three pizzas?
> Who scribbled hearts on the cover of my journal?

However, it isn't always that easy to spot a question. Some are sneaky. They start off like normal sentences:

> It's not raining.
> You like watching TV.

but if you tag a bit on the end, hey presto, they turn into questions:

> It's not raining, is it?
> You like watching TV, don't you?

Are You Asking Or Telling?

Some sentences look as if they should have a question mark, but in fact they don't need one, like these:

He asked if he could leave the table.
The question is whether it's sunny enough for a picnic.

These are known as indirect questions. They describe a question, but they don't actually ask it. To spot an indirect question look out for words such as 'ask' or 'wonder', often followed by 'if', 'when' or 'whether'.

The following sentences both contain the question words ('when' and 'where'), but they're not questions either:

I couldn't decide when to do my homework.
I don't know where my ruler is.

Punctuation Pointer. If a question ends in an abbreviation (see page 94), such as a.m. or p.m., add a question mark, like this:

Do you mean 3 p.m. or 3 a.m.?

Exclamation Marks!

You should use an exclamation mark to highlight a word, phrase or sentence (or for interjections – see page 41). Exclamation marks are a useful way of indicating all sorts of emotions, such as happiness, fear, surprise or pain.

Using exclamation marks in speech shows a shout or a yell. Putting one on the end of words such as 'Ouch!', 'Oh!' and 'Hah!' adds emphasis to what your characters are saying.

If you want to show that someone is bellowing out orders, 'Sit down!' has much more impact than 'Sit down.'

You can use exclamation marks to show sound effects, too – 'Zzzzz!', 'Whoosh!', 'Zoom!' These words will make a comic strip even more exciting:

Watch out though. It's very easy to go too far with exclamation marks – it can even come across as SHOUTING:

'Stop!' shouted the woman. It was no good! The naughty monkey ran off with her hat!

See? Exclamation marks really leap off the page, so if you put in too many your reader will find it distracting, or even annoying, as it's a bit like laughing at your own jokes.

Punctuation Pointer. Think of punctuation marks as a team. Make the exclamation mark sit on the bench most of the time. Only use it when your full stop really needs replacing.

FOR FRIENDS'
_____EYES ONLY ..._____

There's a difference between the writing you do for your teacher and the way you write to your friends. Here are some handy ways you can use exclamation marks in casual writing, but remember, they're not for school work:

> My brother dyed his hair purple (!) today.

Tucking away the exclamation mark in brackets shows what you think. It's a sly little comment on what you've written.

How about an 'interrobang'? An interrobang is a question mark and exclamation mark combined, like this: ?Your teachers will tell you that a sentence cannot have more than one ending — and they're right — so only use this one between friends. It's a fun way of showing that you're astonished and baffled, at the same time:

> My sister wants more homework. Can you believe it?

Remember not to go overboard though — even your best friends will be gnashing their teeth — or snoring — by the time they get to the end of something like this:

> Hi! Thanks for the invite! I'll be round early — so be up!!! Did you decide to invite Keisha after all?! Will she bring Ella?! I hope not! Who else is coming? I need to know!!!

COMMA CORNER

The comma (,) is a tiny mark that packs a punch. It tells you where a sentence needs a short pause, it separates items in a list, and it splits a sentence into 'phrases' and 'clauses' (see pages 47 to 49 for more on these).

Comma Power

By moving, adding or taking away a comma you can change the meaning of a sentence completely. A comma in the wrong place can make things very confusing. You could say:

My favourite foods are fish eggs, and chips.

Or you could say:

My favourite foods are fish, eggs and chips.

However, the first sentence will make everyone think that the eggs that fish lay are one of your favourite foods. That's perfectly fine if they are, but if fish eggs are the last thing you'd like for lunch then you need to think carefully about where to put the comma.

Making Lists

A list of words needs a comma to separate each word from the next, so that:

fish
eggs
chips

becomes fish, eggs and chips. There's no need for a comma either before the first item (fish) or before the word 'and'.

However, if the last two items on your list could be muddled it is best to add a comma, just in case:

I'd like egg, chips, fish and chocolate cake.

A cake made with fish and chocolate would probably be disgusting – add a comma and it becomes much clearer:

I'd like egg, chips, fish, and chocolate cake.

It's up to you whether you think a comma is necessary or not – it also depends on what you want to end up eating.

List Extras

The items on your list don't have to be nouns. You can also make lists of adjectives, such as 'fishy' and 'eggy', or verbs, such as 'to eat' and 'to drink' – in each case, use commas as described above.

Commas can also be used to list groups of words as well as single words. For example:

Today my baby brother scribbled on the kitchen wall, put the cat in the washing machine, broke my pingpong bat and fell asleep in the laundry basket.

Commas For Joining

When you join clauses (see pages 47 to 48), you usually need to put a comma in between them, like this:

My sister likes Hannah, who giggles a lot more than I do.

However, when a clause or phrase gives extra information, you need to put a comma either side of it to split it from the rest of the sentence:

My sister likes Hannah, who giggles, a lot more than I do.

The bit between the commas gives extra information or adds emphasis – you could easily leave out the words inside the commas and the sentence would still be complete. However, the meaning of the second sentence is slightly different to the meaning of the first sentence.

The first sentence says that Hannah giggles more than you and that your sister likes her. The second sentence says that Hannah giggles, but you don't like her as much as your sister does (maybe you find her giggle annoying).

Punctuation Pointer. You sometimes need a comma either side of a name, too, especially when the name is extra information, added for emphasis:

'I, Tarquin Montmorency-Futterbungle, am nine years old.'

'Tell me, Tarquin, are you ever teased about your name?'

PUT IT IN A LETTER

Letter writing is a useful skill, whether you're writing to a friend or applying for your first job.

Addresses

Start by writing your own name and address in the top right-hand corner of the page, with a comma after each line. This way, the person you are writing to will know who the letter is from straightaway.

Punctuation Pointer. Separate each part of a place name with a comma if you are writing a story or an essay, too. For example, you might want to write about Lucy, who lives at Yew Tree Cottage, Old Ford Road, Fordcombe. Each part of the place name tells you more about the location, so your reader knows exactly where you mean.

Letter Writing

Underneath the address, write the date, then start your letter a little way below that on the left. Use 'Dear' then the name of the person you are writing to with 'Mr', 'Mrs', 'Ms' or 'Miss' (unless you are friends, in which case you can use their first name, of course). Add a comma after the name.

Explain what you are writing about in the first paragraph, then go into more detail in the second paragraph. Lastly, finish your letter off by summarizing what you've said and sign off with, 'Yours sincerely,' followed by a comma with your signature underneath.

If you aren't sure of the name of the person you are writing to, start your letter with, 'Dear Sir/Madam,' and sign off with 'Yours faithfully,' instead of 'Yours sincerely,' this time.

Lucy Smith,
Yew Tree Cottage,
Old Ford Road,
Fordcombe

Tuesday 1st April, 1879

Dear Mrs Brown,

I am writing to explain why I won't be coming to dinner tomorrow evening.

It is because I simply can't stand cats and your house is full of them – I'm afraid that I would find the whole evening unbearable and would be terrible company.

I'm very sorry not to be able to come. I do hope that you'll forgive me and that we can still be friends.

Yours sincerely,

Lucy Smith

A Paragraph On Paragraphs

To make your writing easier to read, break it into 'paragraphs'. Each one should be a group of related sentences and you should start a new paragraph when there is a change of subject. Leave a space between paragraphs, as in this book, or 'indent', which means that you start the first line of each one slightly further in from the left to show where it begins.

PUNCTUATING SPEECH

If you are writing a story and want to write down the exact words that someone is saying, it's known as 'direct speech'.

Speech marks (also known as inverted commas, quotation marks or quotes) always come in pairs. You only put them round the words that are spoken.

You can use single speech marks (' ') or double speech marks (" ") for direct speech. Check with your teachers which one they like best and stick with that. These examples all use double speech marks.

Setting Out Speech

Direct speech can be set out with the speech at the beginning, at the end, or even interrupted in the middle of a sentence.

At The Beginning. When the speech comes first, you need a comma inside the speech marks. The comma tells you the speech is finished, and you should take a small pause:

"I want to learn the trombone," said Lauren.

At The End. When the speech comes at the end of the sentence, you need to put a comma before the speech marks. The comma tells you the speech is about to begin, and you should take a small pause:

Lauren said, "I want to learn the trombone."

Interrupted. You can break things up a bit by interrupting a sentence of direct speech. To do this you need a comma inside the first set of speech marks and another comma before the second set. In this case, you don't need to start the second part of the sentence with a capital letter:

"I want," said Lauren, "to learn the trombone."

However, more often than not, you will be able to split the direct speech into two separate sentences, for example:

"I love the trombone," said Lauren.
"I want to learn it."

This means that in most cases, you will need to start the next bit of speech with a capital letter.

Let's Chat

When you are writing a conversation between two or more people, you need to start a new paragraph each time a different person speaks, like this:

"Listening to Lauren's trombone," said Davindra, "is making my ears ache."

"I think she needs more practice," agreed Jack.

Punctuation Pointer. If the speech needs a question or an exclamation mark, you use them in place of a comma or a full stop, inside the speech marks:

"Has she stopped?" Jack asked.

Davindra nodded. "At last!"

Indirect Speech

Instead of writing down the exact words that someone is saying, you can describe what they say without using speech marks at all. This is called indirect speech:

> Dermot said his favourite food was mashed potato.

Indirect speech is useful for factual writing, but if you're telling a story, direct speech is more fun to read – and you can get away with being a lot more casual:

> "What's up?" he said.
> He asked me what was up.

Which do you prefer?

Speech Marks Extras

You can use speech marks in your writing for lots of other things, too:

Quoting. Sometimes, especially in school work, you might need to copy or 'quote' the exact words from a book or newspaper article to back up a point you're making. Put the words you quote in single speech marks to show that they're not your own:

> As Penny Pincher says, 'It is never the right time to ask for a pocket money raise.'

Names. When you are writing by hand, use speech marks if you mention the exact name of something such as a book, film, play, newspaper, song or TV programme, like this:

> At the weekend I watched 'Junior Supercook' on TV. Then I finished my book, 'Storm Island'.

When you are typing on a computer, however, you should put these sorts of words in *italics*.

Special Words. Sometimes it helps to use speech marks to highlight a particular word, like this:

> If you 'sequester' something, it means that you confiscate it.

Being Sarcastic. You can be sarcastic and funny about a word by putting speech marks around it:

> My sister's 'gorgeous' boyfriend is really boring.

The speech marks show you don't agree at all with the true definition of the word. However, remember that some people don't find sarcasm very funny or clever, so they may not appreciate it (especially your sister's boyfriend)!

Double Trouble. Some sentences need two set of speech marks. If that happens, either use single speech marks inside double speech marks, or the other way around. Like this:

> "I went to see 'Haunted Hotel'," said Freya.

or this:

> 'I went to see "Haunted Hotel",' said Freya.

SUPERCOMMA!

The semicolon (;) is a very handy bit of punctuation – it's like a supercomma. Semicolons make a bigger pause than a comma; a smaller pause than a full stop.

A Balancing Act

Use a semicolon when you have two sentences that are linked to each other, but that don't seem quite strong enough to stand alone. They should be equally important, and must be talking about the same thing, for example:

> One juggler was astonishingly skilful; the other juggler was astoundingly clumsy.

Imagine your sentences sitting either end of a seesaw. If the seesaw balances, bring in a supercomma.

Semicolon Lists

You can use semicolons to make a long and complicated list much clearer to read, like this:

In my backpack I stuffed lots of spare clothes in case it rained; some chocolates and sweets; stamps and a pen; and a photo of my cat, Norman.

When each item on the list is several words long – 'lots of spare clothes', 'some chocolate and sweets' and so on – it is much clearer to separate them with semicolons.

In a list that uses semicolons, you are allowed to place a semicolon before the word 'and' when 'and' is bringing in the last item (unlike with a comma list).

Punctuation Pointer. Don't use a semicolon with conjunction words such as 'or', 'but' or 'nor' – look out for these words instead:

however
nevertheless
otherwise
therefore.

A semicolon often works well before them:

The clowns were extremely tired; however, they were determined to finish their performance.

Note that there's no need for a capital letter following a semicolon.

CONQUERING COLONS

A colon (:) can be used to introduce a list, to introduce an explanation, and to introduce speech or quotations – it's a very versatile bit of punctuation.

A List

The first part of the sentence, before the colon, introduces what the list is about. The items on the list follow the colon, with a comma in between each one, except for the last item, which is followed by a full stop. The colon gives you time to pause before the rest of the sentence:

> For the school trip to the Viking museum, you will need: notepad, pens, packed lunch and warm clothing.

An Explanation

A colon can be used to join two sentences when the second sentence explains or adds more detail to the first sentence:

I'm a bit stuck on my Viking project: hopefully the trip to the Viking museum will help.

Speech And Quotations

You can use a colon instead of a comma before speech, like this:

> Jack said: "As it's my birthday, I'd really like a special souvenir from the museum."

You can also use a colon to introduce a quote, like this:

> As the tour guide said: "There's no reason for anyone to be wearing any of the exhibits when they leave."

Punctuation Pointer.
Quite a lot of people have a habit of writing a colon followed by a dash (:–), especially when they are making a list. This isn't allowed!

APOSTROPHE ALERT

Just remember one simple rule: there are only two reasons you ever need an apostrophe ('). One is the 'possessive' – it shows that something belongs. The other shows 'omission' – that letters have been left out. Here's how they work:

One Careful Owner

When you see an apostrophe and a letter **s** at the end of a word, it shows that something belongs to that word, as in:

The cat's pyjamas (the pyjamas belonging to the cat)

and:

The bee's knees (the knees of the bee).

This rule works for any owner – a singular owner. It could be a cat or a bee, or a person or an object, like this.

Jack's book
The book's cover.

If a word ends in a letter **s** already, you still need to add on the **s** after the apostrophe. For example:

The princess's slippers.

Rule-Breakers

If the end of a name is pronounced 'iz' or 'eez', you shouldn't add the extra **s** after the apostrophe – it sounds strange if you do! Examples of words like these include the names Sophocles (pronounced 'sof-o-kleez') and Archimedes (pronounced 'ark-i-meed-eez'). Write them like this:

Sophocles' plays
Archimedes' inventions.

These examples all show possession for singular nouns, but the rules work slightly differently for plurals.

More Than One Owner

When the owner is plural – the boys, the girls, the cats or the bees, for example – the apostrophe goes after the **s**:

That is the boys' dinner
(the dinner belongs to two or more boys).

If a plural, such as 'children', 'men' or 'mice', doesn't end in an **s**, you need to add an apostrophe and an **s**, like this:

the children's playground
the men's ears
the mice's cheese.

Punctuation Pointer. Remember: it makes no difference whether the thing that belongs is singular or plural. Only look at whether the owner is singular or plural to decide where the apostrophe goes.

Vanishing Letters

A 'contraction', when letters are omitted, is something that you use particularly when you are talking. It makes a word shorter and quicker to say. 'Aren't', for example, is short for 'are not' – the two words are joined together, and the **o** in 'not' is removed. An apostrophe is put in place of the **o** to show that it has been removed.

The letter **o** is one of the most common vanishing letters. Here are some more examples:

In Full	Contraction
can not	can't
could not	couldn't
did not	didn't
do not	don't
had not	hadn't
has not	hasn't
is not	isn't
should not	shouldn't
were not	weren't
would not	wouldn't

Rule-Breakers

The following two examples are shortened differently:

shall not	shan't
will not	won't.

Did You Know?

There is an apostrophe in a word that you use every day, whatever time it is – o'clock. In this word, 'of the clock', meaning 'according to the clock', has been shortened.

Common Confusions

The words listed below sound the same but they mean different things. Ask yourself if your sentence has 'is' or 'are' in it, from the verb 'to be', and you'll know that the word needs an apostrophe to replace the missing letter. Here are some examples:

'it's' (it is)
It's time for bed.

'its' (possessive)
The baby wants *its* bed.

'there's' (there is)
There's a rowing boat.

'theirs' (possessive)
Theirs is a blue boat.

'who's' (who is)
Who's going to the park?

'whose' (possessive)
Whose shoes are these?

'you're' (you are)
You're boring me.

'your' (possessive)
Your nose has a spot on it.

Punctuation Pointer. 'Hers', 'his', 'ours', 'theirs', 'yours' ... just like 'its', these possessive pronouns don't need apostrophes. See page 15 for more on possessive pronouns.

Quick Checklist

Each part of the verbs 'to be' and 'to have' can be shortened in the present tense using an apostrophe:

To Be		To Have	
I am	I'm	I have	I've
you are	you're	you have	you've
he is	he's	he has	he's
she is	she's	she has	she's
it is	it's	it has	it's
we are	we're	we have	we've
you are	you're	you have	you've
they are	they're	they have	they've.

Punctuation Pointer. In the future tense (see pages 29 to 30) you use the auxiliary verb 'will'. This is often shortened to - 'll — as in 'I'll', 'you'll', 'she'll', 'they'll', and so on.

'70s Or 1970s?

Apostrophes can be used with numbers to show possession or omission, but never to make a plural. Writing about music *of* the 1970s, you might say:

> The 1970s' songs my grandad loves are really weird.

However, it is more acceptable to use '1970s'.

If you are just writing about the 1970s decade, you can shorten it to '70s with an apostrophe:

> The '70s had lots of weird music my grandad loves.

BRING IN BRACKETS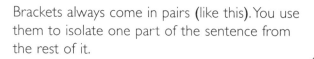

Brackets always come in pairs (like this). You use them to isolate one part of the sentence from the rest of it.

You can use them to explain things, to give opinions and to make an interruption:

> Giraffes are very tall (giants are taller) with long necks.

The useful thing about brackets is that stuff inside them is kept totally separate from the rest of the sentence, which doesn't happen when you use commas:

> Giraffes are very tall, giants are taller, with long necks.

Punctuating Brackets

If the words inside your brackets are a whole sentence, rather than appearing in the middle of a sentence, you should put the full stop inside the brackets, like this:

> My teenage brother is still asleep. (He's been asleep all day.) It's possible he's been enchanted.

If your sentence has a comma in it, place the words in brackets with the part of the sentence they belong to:

> I wanted a doughnut (the oozy, jammy kind), but Mum gave me an apple.

119

DASHES AND HYPHENS

Dashes (–) are a useful replacement for other bits of punctuation, as long as you don't overuse them.

Single Dash

Single dashes can work like commas, semicolons or colons:

I eat fruit almost every day – but I never eat fish.

You can use them to add a bit of suspense or emotion to your writing, like this:

I crept around the corner and
there was – my missing cat!

You can even let speech tail away with a dash, for example:

"I like the new girl, but –" said Emily uncertainly.

Double Dashes

Double dashes work a bit like brackets, and separate one part of a sentence from the rest, like this:

Humpty Dumpty – silly old egg – fell off the wall.

How To Hyphenate

Hyphens (-) look like dashes, but are shorter. However, instead of separating, they join two or more words together to make new words. These are called compound words. The hyphens show that the joined words belong to each other:

son-in-law
green-eyed monster
ten-pound baby

You don't have to use a hyphen for all compound words, but do if you think it makes things clearer. To decide, take a good look at where the words join. Are there lots of letters that you think would look awkward together? Would it look clearer and better with a hyphen? If you think so, put one in. If you don't think so, leave it out. For example, here is a word that can be written with or without the hyphen:

coordinate *or* co-ordinate.

Which do you prefer?

Punctuation Pointer. If you're not sure if the word you are using is one word, two words or if it needs a hyphen, check a dictionary to make sure.

When To Use Hyphens

Use a hyphen if you think your meaning would be unclear without one. For example, it would be easy to misunderstand who was eating who in this sentence:

Beware! Man eating crocodiles!

This is much clearer though:

Beware! Man-eating crocodiles!

Hyphens And Numbers

When you are writing out numbers and fractions that are more than one word you'll need hyphens. For instance, ⅘ becomes four-fifths and 24 becomes twenty-four. Don't go wild though – it's five hundred and forty-eight, not five-hundred-and-forty-eight.

COUNT ON CAPITALS

You know that you need a capital letter at the beginning of a sentence, but there are other times you use a capital letter, too. Use the checklist below to help you put them in the right place.

Punctuation Pointer. When you are writing about yourself, 'I' is always a capital letter – 'me' and 'my' are not.

Capitals Checklist

Names Of People. Always use capitals on the first letter of words when you are writing first names (such as Millie or Jacob), surnames (such as Milton or Jones) and titles (such as Miss and Mr, or Queen or Sir):

> Miss Millie Milton
> Mr Jacob Jones
> Queen Victoria
> Sir Montague Ponsonby-Smythe.

Sometimes titles need a mix of capital and lower-case letters. If you are writing about the President of the United States, for example, 'of' and 'the' don't need capital letters, but the words 'President' and 'United States' do. However, if you are writing about presidents in general, rather than a particular president, there's no need for a capital letter.

The same rule applies to prime ministers, royalty and other important people, too.

Titles. Always use capitals on the first letter of words when you are writing the titles of films, plays, books and TV programmes, like this:

> The Wizard of Oz
> Romeo and Juliet
> The Secret Garden
> Blue Peter.

Notice that, in these cases, you *should* capitalize, 'the' because it is included in the actual titles.

Place Names. The names of places – whether they are the town where you were born, the country you live in or the name of a river or mountain – all need capitals on the first letter of each word, too:

> Fordcombe
> England
> River Combe
> Mount Ford.

Some words such as north, south, east and west are usually lower case, unless they're part of a name – for example, the North Pole and South Korea.

Religious Words. The names of religions, such as Judaism, Christianity, Islam and Buddhism, all need a capital letter at the beginning. And God, Allah, Buddha and other religious names need capital letters, too.

Dates Or Special Days. The names of days, months and festivals or special holidays all need an initial capital letter.

History. If you are writing about events in history, such as the First World War, the Middle Ages or the Battle of Waterloo – you've guessed it – call in the capital letters!

And Finally ...

One last bit of advice, now that you've read about the rules of grammar, spelling and punctuation: keep practising. When you put your knowledge about how to 'write' into practice – whether you're composing a prize-winning poem, writing a thank you letter to a relative, or entering a short-story competition – you're sure to get things 'right'!

INDEX

126

127

Also available ...

Thirty Days Has September:
Cool Ways To
Remember Stuff

ISBN: 978-1-906082-26-0

Off With Their Heads!
All The Cool Bits In
British History

ISBN: 978-1-906082-72-7

I Wish I Knew That:
Cool Stuff You Need
To Know

ISBN: 978-1-907151-10-1

Where On Earth:
Geography Without The
Boring Bits

ISBN: 978-1-907151-16-3